Duties
of Parents

J.C. RYLE

Edited into Modern English by Alan Witchalls

The Duties of Parents
Written by JC Ryle, edited into modern English by Alan Witchalls
© 10Publishing 2012 Alan Witchalls

Published in 2012 by 10Publishing, a division of 10ofthose.com

Unit 9D, Centurion Court, Leyland PR25 3UQ England

Email: publishing@10ofthose.com
Website: www.10ofthose.com

ISBN 9781906173432

Design by Mike Thorpe www.design-chapel.com
Printed in the UK

Contents

DEDICATION

Kirsten my wife, helper and friend
Joshua and Leoni,
you know the way you should go

Foreword

I must confess that despite being a parent of two beautiful children, I have not read many parenting books. This is primarily because I don't like them – they annoy me. I've read the Bible, though, and that seemed sufficient to me.

However, reading topical books can often give us helpful insights and food for thought. A few months before the birth of my first-born son, I started skimming through some parenting books. All I saw was page after page of expert 'opinion' and supposed 'wisdom' that ignored God as the author and director of life, endowed children with saintly innocence, and gave no thought to the reality of death and what may come after it. Hardly any of these books spoke about true parenting: how to bring up our children in 'the training and instruction of the Lord' (Eph. 6:4).

> I must confess that despite being a parent of two beautiful children, I have not read many parenting books... I've read the Bible, though, and that seemed sufficient to me.

This is where J.C. Ryle's booklet *Duties of Parents* stands almost alone in this oversaturated market.

Written over one hundred years ago, the language of this little booklet has become outdated, but the principles it gives us for parenting have not. In the past, when speaking with expectant parents, I would recommend Ryle's booklet to them, but in the back of my mind would be aware of the fact that for some, the language would be hard to understand and therefore put some people off. So, in the spring of 2011, I set about using my spare time to translate the booklet into modern English.

Obviously, this booklet will be most helpful to existing or expectant parents. But this doesn't mean that people without children (or even those with grandchildren) cannot benefit from it. One of my regrets of life pre-children is not spending time observing parents in close quarters and 'practising' at being a daddy in my relationship with the children of close friends. That said, the discussion questions that I have added to Ryle's work are clearly aimed at parents. My hope is that parents (be it individually, with their spouse, or in small groups with other parents) will find these questions helpful as they think about how to apply the principles of parenting in the booklet to their practices of everyday life with their children.

> Just because something is challenging or goes against the grain of our culture does not make it irrelevant or wrong.

While writing, three things have become clear to me. Firstly, it is worth making it clear that the principles in the book are first and foremost those of J.C. Ryle, but I stand behind them wholeheartedly. I have tried to put the content of the booklet into modern English in such a way that will make sense to us in the here and now without losing the essence of what Ryle was originally trying to convey. As I have worked through the booklet, I must admit that it has challenged me and brought me to account with regard to my parenting. There have been a number of instances where I have had to think long and hard about what

Ryle was saying and whether or not I agree with it. This has been a healthy thing for me because I have had to put aside my cultural presuppositions, go back to the Bible and allow it to have the authority over my heart and Ryle's work, not vice versa. Kirsten, my wife, usually observed the greatest change in me and our family as a result of wrestling with these difficult sections. It is also worth noting that J.C. Ryle deserves much credit because in these instances it was my heart that needed correcting, not his work.

> Biblical parenting is timeless and therefore always timely, no matter how uncomfortable it makes us feel

This links to my second observation. A number of the principles in the booklet will be hard to hear and even harder to put into practice. For instance, the chapter entitled *Your Children and Church* will challenge your assumptions on how you parent your children in your church, and the chapter on Your Children and Obedience will stand out as being massively countercultural. But just because something is challenging or goes against the grain of our culture does not make it irrelevant or wrong. J.C. Ryle's work is founded on God's Word from the outset, and is full of biblical principles for parenting. '. . . the word of God is living and active . . . it penetrates even to dividing soul and spirit, joints and marrow' (Heb. 4:12). Biblical parenting is timeless and therefore always timely, no matter how uncomfortable it makes us feel.

Thirdly, it is common for parents to be weighed down with the sheer burden of trying to be 'good' parents. We must always keep in tension our responsibility and God's sovereignty in every

3

aspect of our lives – including our parenting. Our responsibility is to train our children to know and rightly fear Jesus as Lord. God's sovereignty is what actually brings them to know and rightly fear Jesus as Lord – and this is a gift of grace. We mustn't pair one off against the other, or overlook one for the other. We must take our responsibility seriously, repent if need be . . . and leave the rest to God.

If I had to give one criticism of Ryle's original work, it would be that it assumes that the reader knows and understands the heart of the gospel. God is our Father God who loves us and created us to know and love him. The sin of all humankind revealed through Adam and Eve in Genesis 3 ruined that relationship beyond earthly repair – humanity became like a lost son cut off from a loving Father's protection and care. Although it is impossible for us to return to God by ourselves, what is impossible with human beings is possible with God, and so Jesus, the Son of God, came to us. He lived as the perfect Son of Man, took our sin on himself on the cross and rose from the grave to give us eternal life with the Father. Through a living faith in Jesus, our relationship with our heavenly Father is fully restored and will be fully revealed on the last day when Jesus returns to judge the living and the dead. On that day, we get to run into our Father's arms and take our place of honour at a cosmic banquet and feast of such scale that we just simply cannot comprehend it. Until then, we live in his strength through the Holy Spirit who lives in every believer.

> If you want to be a good Christian parent, then start by recognising that you cannot do it – at least not on your own.

If you want to be a good Christian parent, then start by recognising that you cannot do it – at least not on your own. Humble yourself before your heavenly Father and, trusting in all that Jesus has done, ask him to make you into a parent after his own heart through the work of his Spirit in you. Then, by grace, you are free from all condemnation and guilt and can get on with the job of being the parent that Scripture directs you to be.

And so my prayer is that this booklet is easy to understand and is practically useful, while remaining biblically grounded – and therefore honouring to Ryle's original work.

INTRODUCTION: PROVERBS 22:6

Train a child in the way he should go, and when he is old he will not turn from it. (Prov. 22:6)

I suppose that most professing Christians are familiar with the verse above. The sound of it is probably familiar to your ears, like an old tune. It is likely you have heard it or read it, talked of it or quoted it many a time.

But, after all that, how little do we actually listen to what this verse is actually saying to us? The instruction and teaching it contains is apparently not very well known, and unfortunately the duty it places before parents seems rarely put into action.

Just take a look at the world around us, if you think I am not speaking the truth.

The vast majority of children are obviously not trained in the way they should go, for when they grow into adulthood they do not walk with God.

It cannot be said that the subject of 'parenting' is a new one. The world is old, and we have the experience of nearly six thousand years of recorded human history to help us. We live in a day when there is a mighty zeal for education in every area. Government plans for education continue to grow. There are new school developments, new systems and new methods of teaching, new books for children and young people. And of course there is the Internet.

For all this, the vast majority of children are obviously not trained in the way they should go, for when they grow into adulthood they do not walk with God. Now, how shall we account for this state of things? The plain truth is, the Lord's commandment in our text is not being put into practice, and therefore the Lord's promise in our text is not fulfilled.

This may well give rise to a great longing in our heart to know how to best raise our children. Allow then a word of exhortation from a minister about the right training of children. Believe me, the subject is one that should hit home to every conscience, and make every one of us ask ourselves the question, 'Am I doing all that I can in this matter?'

It is a subject that concerns almost all of us. There is hardly a household that it does not touch. Parents, grandparents, carers, childminders, teachers, godfathers, godmothers, uncles, aunts, brothers, sisters – all have an interest in it. There are few people we may be able to think of who might not influence some parent in the management of their family, or affect the training of some child by suggestion or advice. All of us, I suspect, can do something here, either directly or indirectly, and I wish to stir up all of us to bear this matter in our memories.

We will often bring up our children in the very path which we have denounced to our friends as unsafe.

It is also a subject in which all concerned are in great danger of falling short of their duty. This is primarily a point in which we can see the faults of our neighbours more clearly than our own.

We will often bring up our children in the very path which we have denounced to our friends as unsafe. We will see specks of wood in other people's families, and overlook beams of wood in our own. We will be as quick sighted as eagles in detecting the mistakes of others, and yet blind as bats to fatal errors which are daily going on in our homes. We will be wise about how we engage with someone else's family, but foolish about how we treat our own flesh and blood. Here, if anywhere, we have need to question our own wisdom and judgement. This, too, we will do well to bear in mind. [1]

So, let me place before you a few thoughts about right training. I pray that God the Father, God the Son, and God the Holy Spirit bless them and make them words that are helpful and relevant to you all. Don't reject them if you find that they are blunt and simple, and don't ignore them if you find they contain nothing new to you. Be very sure, if we want to raise our children for heaven then these are thoughts that ought not to be lightly set aside.

Discussion Questions

The Bible book of Proverbs often gives us general truths. By this we mean they give us statements that are generally true, instead of ones that are always or especially true. Ultimately, the proverbs in the Bible give us instruction and promises for wise, godly living, but these are always underpinned by complete dependence on God and His sovereignty in our lives.

1. How familiar are you with what Proverbs 22:6 says? Spend a few minutes committing it to memory.

2. From Proverbs 22:6, can you identify . . .

   • the instruction that God gives us in this verse?

   • the promise that God gives us in this verse?

3. What is your self-assessment of your parenting (or involvement in the lives of parents and/or children) to date? Would others (your spouse, your friends, maybe even your children) agree or disagree with this?

4. What is your response to reading this section? Is your response marked by humility and a readiness to engage with Proverbs 22:6, or is your response one of pride and self-justification?

5. How is our parenting linked to our status and acceptance before God? You may find it helpful to look up Romans 3:20–25 and Ephesians 2:8–10.

NOTE

1. Ryle notes: "As a minister, I cannot help remarking that there is hardly any subject on which people seem so tenacious and unable to be challenged on, as they are about their children. I have sometimes been perfectly astonished at the slowness of sensible Christian parents to acknowledge that their own children are at fault, or deserve blame. There are many people to whom I would far rather speak about their own sins, than tell them their children had done anything wrong.'

CHAPTER 1:
THE WAY THEY SHOULD GO

If we would raise our children rightly, we need to train them in the way they should go, and not in the way that they would go.

Remember, children are born with a decided bias towards evil, and therefore if you let them choose for themselves, they are certain to choose wrong. Mothers cannot tell what their tender baby may grow up to be – tall or short, weak or strong, wise or foolish. They may be any of these things; this is all uncertain. But one thing a mother can say with certainty: their child will have a corrupt and sinful heart. It is natural to us to do wrong. Solomon says: 'Foolishness is bound in the heart of a child' (Prov. 22:15, KJV) and 'a child left to himself brings shame to his mother' (Prov. 29:15, NKJV). Our hearts are like the earth on which we tread; leave it alone and it is sure to bear weeds.

If you want to wisely parent your children, then, you must not leave them to the guidance of their own wills.

If you want to wisely parent your children, then, you must not leave them to the guidance of their own wills. Think for them, judge for them, act for them, just as you would for someone who was weak and blind. Whatever you do, don't give them up to their own wayward tastes and desires. It must not be their likings and wishes that are consulted, because they do not yet know what is good for their minds and souls any more than what is good for their body. Just as we decide what is best for them to eat, and what is best for them to drink, and what is best for them to wear, so we should be consistent and deal with their minds in the same way. Train them in the way that is biblical and right, and not in the way that they fancy.

If you cannot make up your mind to this first principle of Christian parenting, it is useless for you to read any further. Self-will is almost the first thing that appears in a child's mind, and it must be our first step to resist it.

Discussion Questions

1. Remind yourself of Psalm 51:5. What does this tell us about the heart of our children, even as mere infants?

2. If you did not teach, instruct and guide your children (and maybe even some teenagers) regarding what they ate, drank or wore, what would happen (think about this in terms of one month, one year, and ten years from now)? Now think about this in terms of what they think and believe. What would their knowledge of and relationship with God be like?

CHAPTER 2:

TENDERNESS, AFFECTION AND PATIENCE

We must train up our children with all tenderness, affection and patience. By this, I do not mean that we should spoil them, but rather that we should let them see that we love them.

Love should be the silver thread that runs through all our conduct. Kindness, gentleness, endurance, restraint, patience, sympathy, a willingness to engage with our child's troubles, a readiness to take part in our child's play – these are the ways by which a child may be led most easily; these are the clues we must follow if we would find the way to their heart. Even among grown-ups, there are not many people who are easier to push in any one direction than there are people who are willing to be brought along with us. In all our minds there is an instinct to forcefully resist compulsion; we get our backs up and stiffen our necks at the very idea of forced obedience. We are like young horses in the hand of a breaker: if handled kindly and made much of, the trainer will be able to eventually guide

> Children are weak and tender creatures and, as such, they need patient and considerate treatment.

them with only a thread; if treated roughly and violently, it will take far longer for the trainer to gain any control over them at all.

Children's minds are cast in much the same mould as our own. A stern and severe manner scares them and sets them back. It closes their hearts, and we will tire ourselves out trying to find a way back in again. But if we let them see that we are truly affectionate towards them – that we really do want to make them happy and do them good, that if we punish them then it is intended for their good, and that, like the pelican, we would give our very blood to nourish their souls – if we let them see this, they will soon be all our own. They must be wooed with kindness, if their attention is ever to be won. Even reason itself teaches us this lesson: Children are weak and tender creatures and, as such, they need patient and considerate treatment. We must handle them delicately and not roughly, like intricate machines, or else we will do more harm than good. They are like young plants that need gentle watering: often, but a little at a time.

> We must remember what children are, and teach them as they are able to bear.

We must not expect everything to change immediately. We must remember what children are, and teach them as they are able to bear. Their minds are like a lump of metal: not to be forged and made useful at once, but instead carefully tapped into shape. Their understanding is like narrow-necked bottles: we must pour in the wine of knowledge gradually, or much of it will be spilled and lost; 'precept upon precept; . . . line upon line; here a little, and there a little' must be our rule (Isa. 23:10). The stone that we use to sharpen a knife does its work slowly, but if we keep on rubbing it, it will bring the blade to a fine edge. Truly, there is need of patience in training a child. Without it, nothing can be done.

Nothing will compensate for the absence of this tenderness and love. A pastor may speak the truth as it is in Jesus: clearly, forcibly, and unanswerably. But if he does not speak it in love, few people will be saved. In the same way, we must set before our children their duty: command, warn, discipline and reason with them. But if we do this without affection, our labour will be in vain.

Love is one grand secret of successful training. Anger and harshness may frighten, but they will not persuade the child that we are right; and if they see us often out of temper, we will soon cease to have their respect. A father who speaks to his son as Saul did to Jonathan (1 Sam. 20:30), should not expect to retain his influence over that son's mind.

Therefore, we need to try hard to keep a hold on our child's affections. It is a dangerous thing to make our children afraid of us. Anything is almost better than formal reserve and harsh constraint between your child and yourself; and this comes about through fear. Fear puts an end to openness in our relationships. Fear leads to concealment. Fear sows the seed of much hypocrisy and leads to many a lie. There is a wealth of truth in the apostle's words to the Colossians: 'Fathers, do not provoke your children, lest they become discouraged'(Col. 3:21, ESV). Let's not overlook the instruction to us as parents in these words.

Discussion Questions

1. Where does your engagement with your children fall on the spectrum between harsh discipline and weak surrender? Do you need to work on bringing more discipline into your child's life (without neglecting love), or bringing more love into your child's life (without neglecting discipline)?

2. Consider the quantity and quality of time spent with your children. Is there anything that you can reasonably do to . . .

   • increase the quantity of time with them?

   • improve the quality of time with them?

CHAPTER 3: OUR CHILDREN'S PRIMARY PASTORS

We must train our children with an ongoing conviction in our minds that much depends upon us as parents.

Grace is the strongest of principles for Christians. See what a revolution grace brings about when it comes into the heart of a sinner: how it overturns the strongholds of Satan, how it casts down the mountains and fills up valleys left by sin in our lives, how it makes crooked things straight – how we become a new creation before God. Truly, nothing is impossible to God's grace. But our sinful nature, too, is very strong. It struggles against the things of the kingdom of God, it fights against every attempt in us to be more holy, and it keeps up an unceasing warfare within us, even to the last hours of our lives.

> But after nature and grace, undoubtedly, there is nothing more powerful in us than how we are brought up as children.

But after nature and grace, undoubtedly, there is nothing more powerful in us than how we are brought up as children. The character we form as infants is, under God, the character that lasts in us and defines us. We are made what we are by training. Our character takes the form of that mould into which our first years are cast. [1]

We depend, in a vast measure, on those who bring us up. We get from them a colour, a taste, a bias which clings to us, more or less, for the rest of our lives. We catch the language of our parents and those that look after us, and we learn to speak it almost without thinking about and questioning it. We catch something of their manners, ways, and attitudes. Only time will show, I suspect, how much we all owe to our early years, and how many things in us may be traced back to seeds sown in our infancy by those who were around us. A renowned seventeenth-century Englishman, John Locke, went as far as to say, '. . . of all the men we meet with, nine parts of ten are what they are, good or evil, useful or not, by their education.' [2]

And all this is one of God's merciful arrangements. He gives our children a mind that will receive impressions like wet clay. He gives them a disposition at the starting point of their lives to believe what we tell them, to take for granted what we advise them, and to trust our word rather than a stranger's. He gives us, in short, a golden opportunity for doing them good. Therefore, make sure that the opportunity is not missed and thrown away. Once let slip, it is gone for ever. Beware of that miserable delusion into which some have fallen: that parents can do nothing for their children, that you must leave them alone,

All this is one of God's merciful arrangements. He gives our children a mind that will receive impressions like wet clay.

wait for God's grace, and sit still. These persons would like them to die the death of a righteous person, but they do nothing to make them live a righteous life.[3] They desire much, and have nothing. And the devil rejoices to see such reasoning, just as he always does over anything which seems to excuse laziness, or to encourage neglect of God's intentions.

I know that you cannot save your child. I know well that anyone who is born again in Jesus is not born of the will of man, but of God. But I also know that God says expressly, 'Train a child in the way he should go' and that God never laid a command on us which He would not then give us grace to perform. And I know, too, that our duty is not to stand still and argue with God, but to go forward and obey God. It is precisely in the going forward that God will meet us. The path of obedience is the way in which He gives the blessing. We have only to do as the servants were commanded at the marriage feast in Cana: to fill the water-pots with water, and then we may safely leave it to Jesus to turn that water into wine. (See John 2:1–11.)

Discussion Questions

As you think about these questions, it is worth reminding yourself of the way the Bible keeps grace and obedience in tension. We parent in God's grace: He saves our children, and He gives us all that we need to parent them. We also parent in obedience to God: we urge our children to walk with Jesus and be saved, and we follow the patterns and principles for parenting that God gives us.

1. What understanding of God, His saving plan in Jesus and the work of the Holy Spirit are your children getting from you as a parent (both explicitly in what you impart to them, and implicitly in what they observe in you)?

2. Where do your children get faithful spiritual nurturing from? Consider what roles the following should play, and are playing in, your children's lives . . .

- **you as parent/s**
- **members of your family**
- **your friends**
- **their friends**
- **your church**
- **the school they go to**

NOTES

1. 'He has seen but little of life who does not discern everywhere the effect of early education on men's opinions and habits of thinking. Children bring out of the nursery that which displays itself throughout their lives.' Richard Cecil, quoted by Ryle. See http://christian-quotes.ochristian.com/Richard-Cecil-Quotes/

2. John Locke, Some Thoughts Concerning Education (London: Printed for A. and J. Churchill, 1693).

3. For instance, in Numbers 23 – 25 and Revelation 2:14 we read of Balaam, who did nothing to prevent the Israelite people from falling into sin, even though he knew full well that God desired the holiness and righteousness of His people.

CHAPTER 4:
YOUR CHILDREN AND JESUS

Raise a child with this thought continually in mind: that the soul of your child is the first thing you must be concerned about.

There is no doubt that our little ones are precious to us. But if we truly love them, then we will be more concerned about their souls and dependence on Jesus than anything else. No other subject should weigh on our hearts and minds more than the subject of their eternity. No part of them should be as dear to us as that part which will never die. The world, with all its glory, will pass away: the hills will melt, the heavens will be rolled up as if they were a scroll, and the sun will cease to shine. But the spirit which dwells in your little child, whom you love so much, will outlive them all. Whether their spirit rests in happiness or misery will, humanly speaking, depend on you.

No other subject should weigh on our hearts and minds more than the subject of their eternity.

It is this thought that should be first and foremost on our minds in all that we do for our children. Think of it in this way: in every step you take with them, in every plan, scheme and arrangement that concerns them, ask yourselves this mighty question: 'How will this affect their soul?'

Love for the soul is the soul of all love. To pander, pamper and indulge our children as if this world was all they had to look to, and this life was the only season for happiness – to do this is not true love, but cruelty. It is treating them as if they were merely an animal, which has only this world to look to and nothing after death. It is hiding from them the greatest truth which ought to be taught to them from their very infancy: that the very purpose of their life is the salvation of their soul.

We must not be ashamed to hear the way we bring our children up being described as 'strange' or 'different'.

If we call ourselves Christians and want to prepare our children for eternity with Jesus in heaven, then we mustn't be slaves to the latest trend, pursuit or fashion. We must not be content to do things merely because it is what everyone else does:

- We must not teach and bring them up in certain ways merely because it is the social norm.
- We shouldn't allow them to read books, browse websites or watch films that are of a questionable sort merely because everybody else reads them, looks at them, or watches them.
- We mustn't let them form unhelpful habits merely because they are the habits of the day.

Instead, we must raise our children with their souls always in mind, even if we face criticism for it. We must not be ashamed to hear the way we bring our children up being described as 'strange' or 'different'. What if it is? The time is short . . . for this world in its present form is passing away (1 Cor. 7:29–31). Parents who prepare their children for heaven, rather than for earth – for God, rather than for human beings – those parents will be called 'wise' in the end.

Discussion Questions

1. What ambitions do you have for your children (think of as many as you can)? Of these ambitions, which will serve them best on the day that they meet Jesus? Which will distract or even tempt them away from living by faith in Jesus?

2. How would you feel if, on the last day, your children's names were not written in Jesus' book of life (the book of who He saves by His grace. See Rev. 20:11–15)?

3. After first reminding ourselves of how we – and our children – are saved (see Eph. 2:8–10), think about how you can use this feeling from question 2 to spur you on to do the following things:

- Regularly pray that our children would repent of their sin and live by faith in Jesus.

- Ensure that our children know the key truths of the gospel.

CHAPTER 5:
YOUR CHILDREN AND THE BIBLE

Train your child to have an understanding of the Bible.

We cannot make our children love the Bible. Only the Holy Spirit can give us a heart that delights in God's Word. However, we can help our children be acquainted with the Bible, and we need to be convicted that they cannot be acquainted with God's great gift of Scripture too soon, or too well.

A thorough knowledge of the Bible is the foundation of all clear views of Jesus, faith in Him and obedience to Him. People who are well grounded in Scripture will generally not be people who waver or doubt, carried about by every wind of teaching. Any upbringing that does not make knowledge of Scripture the first thing is unsafe and unsound. It is vitally important that we understand this, for the devil is at work and there are many erroneous ideas and false theologies out there.

> A thorough knowledge of the Bible is the foundation of all clear views of Jesus, faith in Him and obedience to Him.

For example, some people place a degree of honour, power and authority on the church that should only be reserved for Jesus Christ. There are others who take baptism and communion and make them out to be some sort of spiritual passports that give us access to eternal life. And there are some who honour a certain approach to teaching and parenting more than they do the Bible, being more concerned about filling their child's mind with the tales of irrelevant little storybooks instead of the truth found only in Scripture.

If we love our children then we must let the Bible, plain and simple, be everything in the training of their souls, making sure that all other sources of content (books, music, websites, etc.) are put in their right place of secondary in importance. Think of it like this: don't be so concerned about how good they are at using knowledge, instead be concerned about how good they are at using the Bible. Believe me, this is the approach to raising children that God will honour. In the book of Psalms it says that God has 'exalted above all things [his] name and [his] word' (Ps. 138:2). It makes sense, then, that God would bless all who try to magnify His name and His Word among people.

Make sure that our children read the Bible humbly in the right way.

Here are some thoughts about how to go about getting our children into the Bible:

- Make sure that our children read the Bible humbly in the right way. We should train them to look on it not as the Word of human beings but as it actually is, the Word of God, inspired by the Holy Spirit Himself: totally true, completely profitable, and able to make us wise for salvation through faith in Christ Jesus.

- Make sure that our children read it regularly. We should train them to regard time spent in the Bible as daily food for their soul, being essential to their spiritual health each and every day. Obviously we cannot (and should not) make this anything more than a helpful and healthy habit for our children. But there is no telling how much sin a helpful and healthy habit such as this may indirectly restrain.

- Make sure that our children read it all. We should not shy away from putting any passage or biblical concept before them. Don't be misled into thinking that the key doctrines of Christianity are things which children cannot understand. Children understand far more of the Bible than we give them credit for.

- Make sure that we tell our children about sin, its guilt, its consequences, its power, and its ugliness. We will find that they can comprehend most of these things quite well.

Fill their minds with Scripture. Let the Word of Christ dwell in them richly.

- Make sure that we tell our children about the Lord Jesus Christ and His work in giving us our salvation. Tell them about His atonement for sin, the cross, His blood of the New Covenant, His sacrifice for our sins, and His work of interceding with the Father for us. We will discover that they will grasp something in all of these things.

- Make sure that we tell our children about the work of the

Holy Spirit: how He changes, renews, sanctifies and purifies our hearts and lives.

Our children can keep up with us in all of these things, in one way or another. In short, I suspect we have no idea how much a little child can understand about the greatness of the glorious good news of Jesus. They see far more of these things than we suppose. [1]

Fill their minds with Scripture. Let the word of Christ dwell in them richly. Get them into the Bible, the whole Bible, even while they are young.

Discussion Questions

In 2 Timothy 3:14,15 we see a great example of the role Scripture can have in a child/young person's life. This passage gives us an insight into the early years of Timothy, who was a Christian trained by the apostle Paul, and who eventually became the pastor of the church in Ephesus.

1. Do you think that your child is old enough or mature enough to start engaging with the Bible (either reading it themselves, or with you reading it to them)? Why/why not?

2. What view of Scripture do you think your children have picked up from observing your life? To what extent do you need to apply the things covered in this chapter to your own life first?

3. Take a look back over the list of things about how we engage our children in the Bible.

   • Which of these things are you currently doing well?

   • Which of these things are you currently doing, but could do better at?

   • Which of these things are you not doing at all?

NOTE

1. Ryle notes: " Regarding the age when we should begin teaching our children about Jesus and Christianity, no general rule can be laid down. Some children are able to engage with these things much more quickly than others. Regardless of this, we can seldom begin too early."

CHAPTER 6:
YOUR CHILDREN AND PRAYER

Train them to a habit of prayer.

Prayer is the very life-breath of our walk with God. It is one of the first signs that someone has been born again. "'Go . . .'" Jesus told Ananias, "'and ask for a man from Tarsus named Saul, for he is praying'" (Acts 9:11). Paul had begun to pray, and that was all the proof Jesus needed to give to Ananias. Prayer was the distinguishing mark of the Lord's people in the days when there began to be a separation between them and the world. 'At that time men began to call on the name of the LORD' (Gen. 4:26). Prayer is the peculiar trait of a true Christian. We pray because we tell God our wants, our feelings, our desires, our fears . . . and we mean what we say. A nominal Christian may repeat prayers – and good prayers, too – but they go no further.

When we spend a lot of time with God in prayer, our souls grow like the grass after rain.

Prayer is the turning point in a person's soul. Our ministry is unprofitable and our labour is vain, until we are brought to our knees. Until that happens, we have no hope about us.

Prayer is a great secret of spiritual prosperity. When we spend a lot of time with God in prayer, our souls grow like the grass after rain. When there is little, all will be at a standstill, and you will barely keep your soul alive. Take a look at a growing Christian, a going-forward Christian, a strong Christian, a flourishing Christian, and you can be sure that they are the one that speaks often with Jesus. They ask much and they have much. They tell Jesus everything and so they always know how to act.

Prayer is the mightiest engine God has placed in our hands. It is the best weapon to use in every difficulty, and the surest remedy in every trouble. It is the key that unlocks the treasury of promises, and the hand that draws forth grace and help in time of need. It is the silver trumpet God commands us to sound in all our necessity, and it is the cry He has promised always to attend to, in the same way that a loving mother answers the voice of her child.

Prayer is the simplest means that someone can use in coming to God. It is within reach of everyone: the sick, the elderly, the hospitalised, the paralytic, the blind, the poor, and the uneducated – all of us can pray. We mustn't think that we need to become more experienced, more educated, need to read more, or have a degree in theology before we are able to pray effectively. As long as you have a tongue to tell God about the state of your soul, you can and ought to pray. The words in James 4:2 which say, 'You do not have, because you do not ask God' will be a fearful condemnation to many on the last day.

Parents, if we love our children, we must do all that lies in our power to train them up to a habit of prayer:

- Show them how to begin praying.

- Tell them what to say.

- Encourage them to persevere in prayer.

- Remind them if they become careless and lazy about prayer.

If they choose to never call on the name of the Lord, as terrible as this is, let us make sure that we are not to blame as parents. It is important to remember that prayer is the first step in spiritual discipline that a child is able to take by themselves. Long before they can read, you can teach them to kneel by your side, and repeat the simple words of prayer and praise that you give them. And as the first steps in any undertaking are always the most important, so is the manner in which our children's prayers are prayed. This is a point which deserves our closest attention, for few seem to know how much depends on this. We must be careful not to allow our children to get into a habit of praying in a hasty, careless, and irreverent manner.

Leading our children in prayer mustn't be something we delegate to others (godparents, grandparents, Sunday school teachers or other friends/family). Similarly, we mustn't be too trusting of our children with regard to prayer when left to themselves. Parents who never take ownership of this most important part of their child's daily life simply deserve no praise whatsoever. Surely, if there is any habit at all which parents should be fully involved in developing, it is the habit of prayer. Believe me, if we never hear our children pray, we are much to blame. If this is the case, we are fools like the bird described in Job:

Leading our children in prayer mustn't be something we delegate to others.

She lays her eggs on the ground

and lets them warm in the sand,

unmindful that a foot may crush them,

that some wild animal may trample them.

She treats her young harshly, as if they were not hers;

she cares not that her labour was in vain . . .

(Job 39:14–16)

Prayer is, of all habits, the one which we will remember the longest. There are many grey-headed men and women who could tell you how their parents used to help them pray in the days of their childhood. Other things have faded from their memory – the church where they were taken to worship, the minister whom they first heard preach, the friends who they used to play with – but you will often find it is far different with their first prayers. They will often be able to tell you where they knelt, or what they were taught to say, or even how their mother or father looked whenever they prayed. It will be as fresh in their mind's eye as if it were yesterday.

Reader, if you love your children, I charge you: do not let the time to sow the habit of prayer pass by untouched. If you train your children to anything, train them at least to a habit of prayer.

Discussion Questions

1. How is your own prayer life (individually and, if applicable, as a couple)? As you read the beginning of this chapter, did this speak more to your own habit of prayer than to the habit you are forming in your children?

2. Do we really believe the importance, significance and power of prayer in Jesus' name? Why/why not?

3. What obstacles are in the way of developing habits of prayer in our families? Think (and pray) this through for . . .

   • yourself

   • your husband, wife, or partner (if applicable)

   • your children

CHAPTER 7:
YOUR CHILDREN AND CHURCH

Train them to have a habit of diligently and regularly being part of a church, God's public means of grace.

Tell them of the duty and privilege of being part of a church, and joining in the prayers of the congregation. Tell them that wherever the Lord's people are gathered together, there the Lord Jesus is present in a unique way. It is helpful to remind ourselves that when we are absent from the gathered people of God, we should expect to miss out on something that is a blessing to us. For example, think about the blessing that Thomas almost missed out on because he wasn't with the disciples when they gathered together one Sunday evening – a Sunday that turned out to be the very day that Jesus rose from the dead (John 20:24,25). Tell your children of the importance of hearing the Bible preached, and that it is God's chosen and ordained means for converting, sanctifying, and building up the

> When we are absent from the gathered people of God, we should expect to miss out on something that is a blessing to us.

souls of people. Tell them how the writer of the book of Hebrews encourages us to 'not give up meeting together, as some are in the habit of doing, but let us encourage one another – and all the more as you see the Day approaching' (Heb. 10:25).

It is a sad thing when a church does not have any children in it, except those who only come to the services in order to get a good recommendation so that they can attend the church primary school, or some other such reason. We need to make sure that none of this guilt lies at our doors. There are many children and young people in our neighbourhoods who do not have any connection with a local church, and so we who are their parents and friends should make every effort to ensure that they come with us to church and so experience the joy of God's people gathered together in worship.

We must not allow our children to grow up with a habit of making vain excuses for not coming to church. We need to make it plain to them that as long as they are under our roof it is a family rule that all who are healthy and able will go to church to honour Jesus, who is the head of the church. As harsh as this may seem, our thinking as parents should be as follows: if any of our children choose not to be part of a faithful Jesus-proclaiming church each week then they are, in effect, choosing to murder their own soul.

> We need to understand that the minds of young people are easily distracted, and their attention lost.

Wherever possible, make sure your children come with you to church and sit near you when they are there. To go to church is one thing, but to behave well – and so benefit from being there – is quite another. Believe me, there is no better way of ensuring good behaviour than having them under your own watchful eye.

We need to understand that the minds of young people are easily distracted, and their attention lost. Therefore, every possible means should be used to counteract this. For instance, it is not wise to allow young people to come to church by themselves or to attend a different church than you do. While we would hope that our children and teenagers are able to positively influence each other in these situations, this is certainly not guaranteed. When they are away from us, we have no knowledge or control over who they associate with, and so there is a danger that they will be tempted and led into sin on the very day of the week that is set aside as the Lord's Day.

Likewise, it is not wise to have a clique of young people in a church that completely isolate themselves from the rest of the congregation, either physically or effectually (because of the way the children and/or young people's groups are set up, for example). By being so isolated, they are more likely to be distracted and are at risk of catching habits of inattention and irreverence from their peers – habits which can take years to unlearn . . . if at all. Where possible, it is far better to see whole families sitting together, old and young, side by side – men, women and children, serving God according to their households.

When we turn to the New Testament, we find children mentioned there as joining in public acts of worship.

But there are some who say that it is useless to urge children to attend public means of grace, such as a church, because they cannot understand them.

We must not listen to such reasoning.

For starters, this is not what the Old Testament teaches us. When Moses goes before Pharaoh in Exodus 10:9, we see him saying, 'We will go with our young and old, with our sons and daughters, and with our flocks and herds, because we are to celebrate a festival to the LORD.' When Joshua read the Law to God's people in Joshua 8:35, we see that, 'There was not a word of all that Moses had commanded that Joshua did not read to the whole assembly of Israel, including the women and children, and the [foreigners] who lived among them.' Lastly, in Exodus 34:23 the Israelites are told, 'Three times a year all your men are to appear before the Sovereign LORD, the God of Israel.' The word 'men' literally means 'all males' or 'men-children'.

So parents, comfort your hearts and minds with these examples across the history of God's people.

Likewise, when we turn to the New Testament, we find children mentioned there as joining in public acts of worship in the same way as in the Old Testament. When Paul was leaving the disciples at Tyre for the last time (Acts 21:5), we see it reported that 'All the disciples and their wives and children accompanied us out of the city, and there on the beach [they] knelt to pray.'

Furthermore, as we examine Scripture we see examples of people worshipping and serving God who did not possess a full understanding of Him. The Old Testament prophet Samuel, in the days of his childhood, appears to have served the Lord quite some time before he really knew Him: 'The boy Samuel ministered before the LORD under Eli . . . Now Samuel did not yet know the LORD: The word of the LORD had not yet been revealed to him' (1 Sam. 3:1,7). Even the apostles themselves did not seem to have understood all that Jesus said to them at the time: 'At first his disciples did not understand all this. Only after Jesus was glorified did they realise that these things had been written about him and that they had done these things to him' (John 12:16).

So parents, comfort your hearts and minds with these examples across the history of God's people. Don't feel downcast because your children do not see the full value of church as a means of grace now. Simply train them up to a habit of regular attendance. Establish it in their minds as a high, holy and important part of their life. If we do this, then the day will very likely come when they will bless you for it.

Discussion Questions

1. What is your own attitude to attending church regularly and being an active member of the fellowship? What influence or impact is this having on your children?

2. What things prevent a) your whole family going to church, and, b) your whole family going to church every week? What can you do about these things?

3. In light of what you have read in this chapter, think about whether or not the following things should affect whether or not your children attend and are part of your church:

- How much they understand everything that happens.

- How much they want to be there.

- How tired they are or how busy the weekend has been.

- How much schoolwork they have to do.

NOTE

1. This also has the added advantage of providing a natural and secure context for children or teenagers to be a part of the church where they either have parent/s that do not go to church, or they come from a broken home. For instance, children or teenagers who visit or attend church with a Christian friend and his or her family need to be seen as extended members of that Christian family. Therefore, parents should see it as their privilege and responsibility to look after the visiting child or teen and include them in the life of the church as part of their family. Similarly, families need to be looking out for and welcoming new or visiting teenagers who are at the church on their own. As a relatively new believer, I (Alan) began attending a new church by myself in my late teenage years. I am extremely grateful for the way that other young people my age welcomed me and their families looked out for me and made me feel part of the church by including me in their everyday lives (inviting me round for Sunday lunch and things like that).

CHAPTER 8:
YOUR CHILDREN AND TRUSTING YOU

Train them to a habit of faith.

By this I mean that we should train them up to believe what we say. We should try to give our children a confidence in our judgement and a respect for our opinions as being better than their own. Get them used to thinking that when you say a thing is bad for them, then it must be bad. Likewise, when you say it is good for them, then it must be good. Help them to understand that your knowledge, in short, is better than their own and, therefore, that they may rely implicitly on what you say. Give them the assurance that what they don't yet know or understand now, they will probably know and understand in the course of time, and that in the meantime they can be sure there is a reason for everything you require them to do.

It is hard to describe how reassuring a real spirit of faith can be. Or, to look at it another way, it is hard to describe just how much uncertainty and worry unbelief has brought upon the world. Unbelief made Eve eat the forbidden fruit – she doubted the truth of God's word when he said, 'you will surely die' (Gen.

2:17). Unbelief made the world of old reject Noah's warning and so perish in the flood because of their sin. Unbelief kept Israel in the wilderness, even after God parted the water and led them through the sea – in the end it was the barrier that kept them from entering the Promised Land. Unbelief made the Jews crucify Jesus, the very Son of God – they chose not to believe the voice of Moses and the prophets in the Old Testament, even though they were read to them every day. And unbelief is the reigning sin of the human heart down through the ages to this very day: unbelief in God's promises, unbelief in God's warnings, unbelief in our own sinfulness, unbelief in our own danger, unbelief in everything that addresses the pride and worldliness of our evil hearts. Friends, we train our children for nothing if we do not train them to a habit of implicit faith – faith in our word as their parents, and confidence that what we say must be right.

Friends, we train our children for nothing if we do not train them to a habit of implicit faith.

Some people say that you should require nothing of children which they themselves cannot understand, and that you should explain and give a reason for everything you desire them to do. We must be very careful of such thinking. Indeed, it is an unsound and damaging principle. Obviously, it would be wrong to leave them in the dark, so to speak, and never explain anything to our children. There are many things that we should explain, in order that they may see that these things are reasonable and wise. But to bring them up with the idea that they should take nothing on trust and that they, with their immature and imperfect understanding must have the 'why' and 'wherefore' made clear to them at every step they take is indeed a fearful mistake which is likely to have the worst effect on their minds.

Reasoning with our children can be a wise and helpful thing to do, at certain times. But we should never lose sight of the fact that our children are still only children, after all – that each of them thinks as a child, understands as a child, and therefore (if we truly love them) must not be expected to act like an adult who knows and understands the reason of everything at once.

We should never lose sight of the fact that our children are still only children, after all.

A good example to set before them is the example of Isaac. On the day when Abraham took him to offer him on Mount Moriah (Gen. 22), he asked his father a single question: 'Where is the lamb for the sacrifice?' He got no answer but this from Abraham: 'God will provide a lamb.' How, from where, or when, or in what manner, or by what means this lamb was going to be provided was not told to Isaac; yet the simple answer was enough. He believed that all would be well because his father had said so, and so he was content. Therefore, tell your children everyone must learn the basics to begin with, that in every area of knowledge we must start with the simple things, the ABCs. Even the best horse in the world started out needing to be broken. And encourage them that a day will come when they will see the wisdom of all your training.

But in the meantime, if you say a thing is right, then it must be

45

enough for them, they must believe you, and be content.

Parents, if any point in training is important, it is this. I charge you by the affection you have for your children, use every means to train them up to a habit of faith – taking you at your word because you love them.

Discussion Questions

In our culture, faith is often used as an abstract concept – 'just have faith'. In this chapter, faith is referred to in a very concrete sense: it is faith in something or someone, namely you as parents (or carers), who are their God-given overseers.

1. **What degree of faith do your children have in you at present? For instance, how do your children react when you give them an instruction or command?**

2. **What can you practically do to instil in your children a right trust in your word?**
   * **What will you do when they do trust/obey you?**
   * **What will you do when they do not trust/obey you?**
   * **What will you do when you make a mistake and get it wrong?**

3. **How will helping our children trust us as their parents or guardians impact them in their relationship with their heavenly Father?**

CHAPTER 9:
YOUR CHILDREN AND OBEDIENCE

Train them to a habit of obedience.

This is a goal which is worth any amount of effort to achieve. There is no other habit, I suspect, that has such an influence over our lives as this. Parents, be thoroughly determined that your children will obey you, even though it may cause you much trouble . . . and cost them not a few tears! Even though this is massively countercultural, let there be no questioning, no reasoning, no disputing, no delaying, and no answering back. When you give them a command, let them see plainly that you will have it done.

> Parents, be thoroughly determined that your children will obey you, even though it may cause you much trouble.

Obedience is the only reality. It is faith visible, faith acting, and faith embodied. It is the test of real discipleship among the Lord's people. 'You are my friends if you do what I command' (John 15:14). Because of this, it ought to be the mark of well-trained children that they do whatever their parents command them. The fifth commandment urges children to honour their father and mother (see Exod. 20:12; Deut. 5:16; Eph. 6:1–3). How else other than through children obeying their parents cheerfully, willingly and at once, can this honour be given to them?

Early obedience of children can be found throughout the whole Bible. Abraham was praised not only for the fact that he would bring up his children, but that he would 'direct his children and his household after him' (Gen. 18:19). Likewise, Luke 2:51 tell us that the Lord Jesus Himself was obedient to Mary and Joseph.

In Genesis 37:13 we see Joseph obeying his father, Jacob. Isaiah 3:5 tells us that it is an evil thing when the young 'rise up against the old'. The apostle Paul includes disobedience to parents as one of the negative signs of the last days (2 Tim. 3:2). Paul also singles this out as a key requirement of a Christian minister: 'He must manage his own family well and see that his children obey him with proper respect' (1 Tim. 3:4). This is also applied to deacons in the same way: 'A deacon . . . must manage his children and his household well' (1 Tim. 3:12). Lastly, a church elder must be 'a man whose children believe and are not open to the charge of being wild and disobedient' (Titus 1:6).

Parents, if we love our children, then let obedience be an expectation.

Parents, do we wish to see our children happy? We must take care, then, that we train them to obey when they are spoken to – essentially, to do as they are told. We are not made for independence; we are simply not fit for it. Even people who have been set free by Jesus are now bound to Him, because 'It is the Lord Christ [we] are serving' (Col. 3:24). Children cannot learn too soon that this is a world in which we are not all intended to rule, and that we are never in our right place until we know how to obey those in authority over us. We need to teach them to obey while young, or else they will be pulling against God for the rest of their lives and wear themselves out with the vain idea that they are independent of His control.

This aspect of parenting is very much needed. You will see many in this day and age who allow their children to choose and think for themselves long before they are able, and even end up making excuses for their disobedience, as if this were something beyond their control. A parent who is always yielding to their child, and a child who is always having their own way, is a most painful sight. It is painful because we see God's appointed order of things inverted and turned upside down. It is painful because the consequences to that child's character in the end will be self-will, pride and self-conceit. We mustn't be surprised that people refuse to obey their heavenly Father if we allow them, when they are children, to disobey their earthly father. (If they do not have a father at home, a good, strong male role model can help to teach them respect and authority.) [1]

Parents, if we love our children, then let obedience be an expectation and a core belief that we put continually before their eyes.

Discussion Questions

1. What is your expectation of obedience in your children? How have you formed this expectation, and how does this compare with the expectations and exhortations given to us in Scripture?

2. Do you believe the promise of the fifth commandment to honour parents (see Eph. 6:1–3)?

   • In what ways does obedience generally result in things 'going well' for our children?

   • In what ways does obedience generally result in 'long life on the earth' for our children?

3. What one area of obedience does your child need to grow in? What steps are you going to take to encourage obedience in this area?

NOTE

1. For the fathers and men in our churches, there is an implicit call here to be loving, godly and strong male role models for the children and teenagers in our fellowships who, for whatever reason, do not have a father at home. Such children need to see the loving care and concern of our heavenly Father displayed through their relationships with multiple father figures in the church.

CHAPTER 10:
YOUR CHILDREN AND THE TRUTH

Train them to a habit of always speaking the truth.

Speaking the truth is a trait that is far less common in the world today than we might first think. We are familiar with the phrase: 'the whole truth and nothing but the truth'. But these are words that many of us would do well to bear in mind. Lying and distorting the truth are old sins, and the devil was the father of lies: he deceived Eve by a bold lie, and ever since the Fall it has become a sin against which all of humankind need to be on their guard.

Just stop for a minute and think about how much falsehood and deceit there is in the world. Think about how much people exaggerate when telling a story, or how people add to the 'truth'? More importantly, think about the things that are left out . . . if it does not serve the speaker's interest to include them. When you think of all the people you know, how many of them would you be able to say that you trust their every word? In ancient Persia, young men were carefully taught in three simple things: to ride, to draw the bow, and to speak the

We need to remind ourselves of how often God is spoken of in the Old Testament as the God of truth.

truth. It is worth noting how that generation of Persians were indeed very wise. But what an awful proof of humanity's natural sinfulness this is that we should need to point out such wisdom in the first place.

We need to remind ourselves of how often God is spoken of in the Old Testament as the God of truth. Indeed, as we read Scripture it is clear that truth seems to be especially set before us as a leading trait in God's character. God never swerves from the straight line of truth. He abhors lying and hypocrisy.

This is something that we need to try to keep continually in our children's minds. We need to impress upon them at all times that anything less than the truth is a lie; that evasion, excuse-making, and exaggeration are all halfway houses towards what is false, and therefore ought to be avoided. We must encourage them in any and every circumstance to be straightforward and, whatever the cost, to speak the truth.

> We must encourage them in any and every circumstance to be straightforward and, whatever the cost, to speak the truth.

This subject demands our attention, not merely for the sake of our children's character in the world, but for the sake of our dealings with them as their parents. As we bring up our children, we will find it a great help indeed to be able to always trust their word. This will go a long way to prevent the habit of concealing the truth, which is sometimes prevalent among kids. Our openness and truthfulness as adults depends a great deal on how our parents brought us up in this matter as children.

Discussion Questions

1. To what degree do you model truth-telling and honesty to your children? Do they trust your every word?

2. Think of the people you know who you regard as truthful. What characterises their honesty, and how might you use this to shape your children?

3. Children have a tendency to be ready to 'tell the truth' on others, but not so keen when it comes to their own words or actions. What can we do in such situations to encourage truth-telling?

CHAPTER 11:
YOUR CHILDREN AND IDLENESS

Train them to a habit of making use of time.

Idleness is the devil's best friend. It is the surest way to give him an opportunity to do us harm. An idle mind is like an open door, and if Satan himself does not enter in by it, then you can be sure he will throw in something else to raise bad thoughts in our souls.

No created being was ever meant to be idle. Service and work is the appointed portion of every creature of God. The angels in heaven work – they are His servants, ever doing His will. Adam, in the Garden of Eden, had work to do – he was given the task of tending and looking after the garden. All who are brought into the glory of the new heavens and the new earth will have work to do: 'they are before the throne of God and serve him day and night in his temple' (Rev. 7:15). And so now, as weak sinful people, we must have something to occupy our time, or else we will soon find ourselves in a spiritually unhealthy state. We must put our hands to work and keep our minds occupied, or else our imaginations will soon ferment and breed mischief.

Service and work is the appointed portion of every creature of God.

What is true of us is also true of our children. We should feel

55

sorry for someone who has nothing to do. The people of the Old Testament thought that idleness was a definite sin: it was a law of theirs that every man should bring up his son in a useful trade. They knew the heart of humanity better than some of us appear to.

There are plenty of examples in Scripture. For instance, in Ezekiel we find that it was idleness that made Sodom the sinful place it was: 'Now this was the sin of your sister Sodom: She and her daughters were arrogant, overfed and unconcerned (literally 'abundant in idleness'); they did not help the poor and needy' (Ezek. 16:49). Idleness had much to do with David's terrible sin with the wife of Uriah. We read in 2 Samuel 11 that it was 'the time when kings go off to war', yet it was Joab that went out to war against Ammon, while 'David remained in Jerusalem' (v. 1). Was that not idleness? It was only at this point that he saw Bathsheba . . . and the next step we read of is his tremendous and miserable fall.

> The active, moving mind is a hard mark for the devil to shoot at.

Truly, I believe that idleness has led to more sin than almost any other habit that could be named. I suspect it has been responsible for many a work of the flesh: adultery, fornication, drunkenness, and many other deeds of darkness. Let your own conscience decide whether I do not speak the truth. Think about the times that you have fallen into sin. How many times was this because you were idle, and at once the devil knocked at the door and came in?

It is amazing that nearly everything in the world around us seems to teach us this same lesson. It is the still water which becomes stagnant and impure; whereas the running, moving streams are always clear. If you have an engine or machinery, you must work on it, service it and keep it well maintained, or it soon gets out of order. If you own an animal such as a dog or maybe even a horse, you must exercise them. They are usually at their healthiest and fittest when they have regular exercise and are kept active. If you want to be healthy and fit yourself, you must take time to exercise or go to the gym and work out. If you always sit still, your body is sure to suffer. And so it is with the soul. The active, moving mind is a hard mark for the devil to shoot at. Try to find useful ways to keep yourselves active and engaged in work, service or helpful pastimes. If we do this, the enemy will find it hard to find room to sow seeds of sinfulness in our lives.

If we would train our children wisely, we must carefully note how God the Father trains us, His children.

In the same way, it is important that we set these things before the minds of our children. We need to teach them the value of time, and try to help them learn the habit of using it well. It pains me to see children wasting their time or not really caring about what they are doing. I love to see them active and industrious, giving their whole heart to all they do: giving their all in lessons when they are at school, and giving their all when they are playing at home or with friends.

If we indeed love our children, we will make sure that idleness is counted as a sin in our families.

Discussion Questions

1. Are you/your children prone to idleness, or overwork? Why do you think this is, and what can you do about it?

2. What things in our lives and the lives of our children draw us into being idle? In particular, think:

   • What do you need to stop doing?

   • What do you need to change?

   • What do you need to start doing?

CHAPTER 12:
YOUR CHILDREN AND BEING SPOILT

Train your children with a constant fear of overindulging them.

This is the one crucial point we need to be on our guard against, especially in our Western culture. It is natural for us to be tender and affectionate towards our own flesh and blood, and it is the excess of this very tenderness and affection of which we have to beware. We need to make sure that it does not make us blind to our children's faults, and deaf to any advice about them. We must heed this warning out of fear of choosing to overlook bad conduct rather than have the pain of inflicting punishment and correction.

We all know very well that punishment and correction are not pleasant things. Nothing is more unpleasant than upsetting those we love, especially when the tears start to flow. But as long as hearts are what hearts are – stained and corrupted by sin – it is futile to think that children can ever be brought up without correction.

'Spoiling' a child is a very expressive phrase, and one that is unfortunately full of meaning. The quickest way to spoil children is to let them have their own way: to allow them to do wrong and not to punish them for it. We must not let this happen, no matter what pain it may cost us, unless we wish to ruin our children's souls.

We cannot even say that the Bible does not speak expressly on this subject:

> *He who spares the rod hates his son, but he who loves him is careful to discipline him.* (Prov. 13:24)

> *Discipline your son, for in that there is hope; do not be a willing party to his death.* (Prov. 19:18)

> *Folly is bound up in the heart of a child, but the rod of discipline will drive it far from him.* (Prov. 22:15)

> *Do not withhold discipline from a child; if you punish him with the rod, he will not die. Punish him with the rod and save his soul from death.* (Prov. 23:13,14)

> *The rod of correction imparts wisdom, but a child left to himself disgraces his mother. . . . Discipline your son, and he will give you peace; he will bring delight to your soul.* (Prov. 29:15,17)

How strong and forcible are these verses! Yet how sobering is it that in many Christian families these verses of the Bible seem almost unheard of. Our children need reproof, but it is hardly ever given. They need correction, but it is hardly ever employed. And yet the book of Proverbs is not obsolete and unfit for Christians. It is given by the inspiration of God, and is

Put plainly and simply, if we never punish our children when they are at fault then we are doing them a grievous wrong.

therefore profitable for us in everyday life. Proverbs is given just as much for our spiritual good as Romans or Ephesians. Surely anyone who brings up their children without paying careful attention to its wisdom is putting themselves above God's wisdom in Scripture, and therefore making a grave mistake.

Put plainly and simply, if we never punish our children when they are at fault then we are doing them a grievous wrong. Pandering to our children is the rock on which the saints of God, in every age, have only too frequently been shipwrecked upon. I would urge you to be wise about this ahead of time, and so keep clear of failing into this trap.

Here's an example from the Bible. In the Old Testament we see a priest named Eli, and his sons, Hophni and Phinehas, who 'made themselves contemptible, and he failed to restrain them' (1 Sam. 3:13). Eli gave them no more than a tame and lukewarm telling off, when he ought to have rebuked them sharply. To put it simply, he honoured his sons above God (1 Sam. 2:22–29). And what

We should seek to train them, not to humour them; to help them grow, not merely to please them.

was the result of these things? Eli lived to hear of the death of both his sons in battle, and died the same day (4:17,18).

We find another example for us in the case of David and his sons. Amnon's incest, Absalom's murder and proud rebellion, Adonijah's scheming ambition . . . truly these were grievous wounds for David – the man after God's own heart – to receive from his own household. But was there no fault on David's part? I fear there can be no doubt there was. We find a clue to it all in the account of Adonijah in 1 Kings 1:6: 'His father had never interfered with him by asking, "Why do you behave as you do?"' This was the foundation of all the trouble that followed. David was an overindulgent father – a father who let his children have their own way – and he reaped according to what he had sown.

Parents, for the sake of our children, we must beware of overindulgence. Remember, it is our first duty to look after their real interests and not their wants or desires. We should seek to train them, not to humour them; to help them grow, not merely to please them.

We must not give way to every wish and whim of our child's mind, however much we may love them. We must not let them suppose that their will is the be-all and end-all, that they have only to desire something and it will be done. Whatever we do, we must not make our children into our idols, in case our holy and jealous God should need to take drastic action to convince and convict us of our idolatry and foolishness.

> We must not give way to every wish and whim of our child's mind, however much we may love them.

Learn to say 'no' to your children. Show them that you are able to refuse whatever you think is unfit for them. Show them that you are ready to punish disobedience, and that when you speak of punishment, you are not only ready to threaten it but also to carry it out. Yet, do not threaten too much. [1] There is an old saying, 'Threatened men live long', which essentially highlights how we soon realise when threats against us are hollow and rarely get carried out. So, seldom punish your children, but when you do, do it properly and in earnest because frequent and insignificant punishments are just as ineffective as no punishment at all. [2]

Beware of letting small faults pass unnoticed under the idea 'it just a small thing'. There are no small things when raising children – all are important. Small weeds need plucking up as much as the big ones, because if you leave them alone, they will soon grow bigger and bigger. If there is any point which deserves your attention – especially in our present Western culture of pandering to children – then it is this one. To be sure, doing these things will be difficult. But if we do not face difficult things with our children when they are young, then they will be far more difficult when they are older. Choose which you prefer.

Discussion Questions

1. On a scale of one to ten (one being not at all, and ten being too much), how often do your children get their own way?

2. What is your view on discipline for your children? Is your view formed from Scripture, or from the world-view of those around you?

3. What one thing can you do to better discipline your child/children? Take some time to think about each child individually.

NOTES

1. Ryle notes: "Some parents and carers have a way of saying, 'Don't do that' to their boy or girl for every little thing, and often without good reason. This is a very foolish habit to get into. Words of blame should never be used without real reason."

2. Ryle notes: "As to the best way of punishing a child, no general rule can be laid down; the characters and personalities of children are so exceedingly different. What would be a severe punishment to one child would be no punishment at all to another. I only wish to raise a clear protest against the modern notion that no child ought ever to be punished or disciplined, whether verbally or physically. Doubtless some parents use physical punishment far too much, and sadly far too violently. But many others, I fear, use it far too little."

CHAPTER 13: REMEMBER GOD'S EXAMPLE

Train them, remembering continually how God trains His children.

The Bible tells us that God has a chosen people: His family in this world. All sinners who have been convinced of their sin and have fled to Jesus for forgiveness and peace with God now make up His family. All of us who really believe in Jesus for our salvation are members of it.

At present, God the Father is constantly training the members of His family, preparing them for eternity with Him in the kingdom of heaven and the new creation. He acts like a gardener pruning His vines so that they may bear more fruit.

God knows the character of each of us: our habitual sins, our weaknesses, our particular struggles, our special needs. He knows what we do and where we live; who are our friends and companions in life; and what are our trials, temptations, and strengths. He knows all these things and is continually ordering and arranging them for our good. He gives to each of us, in His providence, the very things we need in order to bear the most fruit. Imagine we are branches

At present, God the Father is constantly training the members of His family.

on a vine. God gives us as much sunshine as we can stand, and as much rain as we need. God gives us as much of the bitter things in life as we can bear, and as much of sweet things in the same way.

And so, if we would train our children wisely, we must carefully note how God the Father trains us, His children. God does all things well, and so the way in which He goes about training and nurturing His family must be the right one.

As we look at God's plan for raising children, the first thing we see is just how often God withholds something from His children. I suspect that there are very few people in Scripture who have had a desire that God fulfilled straight away, without hesitation. Often we see God's people desiring something yet unable to get it, as if God were placing it above their reach, saying, 'No. This is not good for you, this must not be.' For instance, Moses strongly desired to cross over the River Jordan into the promised land of Canaan, yet his desire was never granted.

If we would train our children wisely, we must carefully note how God the Father trains us, His children.

The next thing we see is how often God leads His people by ways which seem strange and mysterious to us. We cannot usually see or understand the purpose behind all His dealings with us. Likewise, we cannot usually see the reason why we are following the particular path that God has led us down. Sometimes, there are so many trials that we are faced with, so many difficulties around us, yet we are unable to discover the meaning behind it all. It is as if our Father was taking us by the hand into a dark place and saying, 'Ask no questions. Just follow Me.' Think of the people of Israel after the Exodus. There was a direct road from Egypt to the Promised Land; yet, because of their disobedience, Israel was not led straight into it. Instead, they were led round through the wilderness for forty years. This must have been hard for the people of Israel at the time, who 'grew impatient on the way' (Num. 21:4), yet God was teaching His people the lesson of trusting Him completely.

One other thing we see is how often God disciplines His people using trials and affliction. In Scripture we see Him sending disappointments, and giving them crosses to bear. He allows them to be laid low with sickness, He strips them of property and friends, He moves them from one place to another, and He comes to them with things that are physically hard to bear. For some of us, we have experienced these things ourselves and perhaps have nearly collapsed under the burdens upon us. We have felt pressed beyond our strength, and have been almost ready to disown God and speak out against the One which has allowed these things to be. The apostle Paul, for instance, had a thorn in the flesh appointed to him. Although we do not know exactly what this was, it is a fair assumption to make that this was some terrible bodily trial or illness. Whatever it was, we know that he pleaded with the Lord three times that it might be removed, and yet it was not taken away. Instead he was told: 'My grace

Do not be afraid to withhold from your child anything you think will do them harm, whatever their own wishes may be.

is sufficient for you, for my power is made perfect in weakness' (2 Cor. 12:8,9).

Even if we put all these examples in Scripture aside, has there ever been a single believer and child of God who truly thought at the end of the day that their Father in heaven did not treat them wisely? No, I am sure there has not. Although many of us may have had our faith sorely tested in this, and may even have cried out to God about the apparent unfairness of life, God's children will always tell you that in the long run, it was a good thing that they did not have their own way, and that God has done far more for them than they could have done for themselves.

> We must not forget that children learn more by what they see than what they hear.

More than that, they will tell you that God's dealings have provided more blessing and happiness for them than they ever could have obtained for themselves, and that His way – however dark and difficult it may seem at the time – was the way of blessing and the path of peace.

I urge you to take to heart the lesson which God's dealings with His people teaches us. Do not be afraid to withhold from your child anything you think will do them harm, whatever their own wishes may be. Remember, this is God's plan for raising children.

Do not hesitate to give them commands to obey, even though they may not be able to see the reason why at the present time. Guide them rightly in life, even if they think you are being unfair or unreasonable. This is God's plan for raising children.

Don't shy away from rebuking and correcting your children

whenever they need it, however painful it may be. Think of your discipline as being good for their soul's health. In the same way that we do not refuse to give our children medicine just because it might taste bad, so we do not refuse to give our children discipline just because it might be unpleasant to them. Remember, this is God's plan for raising children.

Lastly and most importantly, do not be worried or concerned that following God's plan might make them unhappy. Let me warn you against this delusion. We must hold fast to this truth: there is no road more certain to lead to unhappiness than always having our own way. To have our desires checked and denied is a blessing for us, not least because it makes us value them when they do come our way. To be constantly indulged is the way to be made selfish – and selfish, spoiled children are seldom happy.

So I urge you not to think of yourself as being wiser than God: raise your family in the same way that God raises His.

Discussion Questions

1. Read Hebrews 12:4–11. Make a note of what it says about . . .

   a) How God treats His children.

   b) How parents (fathers in particular) are expected to treat their children.

2. What aspect of your parenting is most out of line with our heavenly Father's example? Spend time asking the Holy Spirit to shape you to be more like God in your parenting.

3. How would you complete this sentence: 'A great father/mother is someone who . . .' How would Jesus finish this sentence?

CHAPTER 14:
REMEMBER
YOUR EXAMPLE

Train them remembering continually the influence of your own example.

The instructions, advice, and commands that we give our children will do little good unless they are backed up in our own lives, too. For as long as our actions contradict our instructions, our children will never believe we are sincere in our intentions for them to obey us.

John Tillotson, a seventeenth-century archbishop, wisely commented that 'To give children good instruction, and a bad example, is but beckoning to them with the head to show them the way to heaven, while we take them by the hand and lead them in the way to hell.' [1]

We are often unaware of the force and power that our example has over others. No one can live an isolated life that does not have some sort of impact on someone else. In one way or another, we are always influencing those around us – whether for good or for evil, whether in godliness or in sinfulness. Those around us see our ways, they note our conduct, they observe our behaviour. What they see us

> No one can live an isolated life that does not have some sort of impact on someone else.

doing, they may fairly suppose, is what we believe is the right thing to do. This is especially the case with parents and their children.

As parents, we must not forget that children learn more by what they see than what they hear. The impact that going to school has on our children is insignificant compared to the impact of their family. The best of teachers will not be able to imprint on their minds as much as they will pick up from us at home. Imitation is a far stronger principle with children than committing things to memory, and what they see has a much stronger effect on their minds than what they are told.

Therefore, we must be mindful of what we do in front of our children. There is a saying which speaks the truth about this matter: 'Who sins before a child, sins double.' So, we must strive rather to be a living depiction of Jesus that our families can clearly and plainly understand. Be an example of reverence for the Word of God, prayer, the means of grace (baptism and communion), and for taking the Lord's Day as time out. Be an example with your language, your temper, your diligence, your moderation with things such as alcohol, your faith, your charity and generosity, your kindness, your humility. Don't make the mistake of thinking that your children will put into practise things that they do not see you doing. You are their role model, and they will copy what you are. Your children might not be able to fully understand the things you teach, your wise

We must strive to be a living depiction of Jesus that our families can clearly and plainly understand.

commands and your good advice, but they can understand your life.

Children are very observant indeed: they are quick in seeing through most of our hypocrisy, quick in finding out what we really think and feel, quick in adopting all our ways and opinions. For this reason, people often say 'like father, like son'.

In the Roman world, whenever Caesar went into battle with his soldiers, he did not say 'Go forward!' but 'Come!' So it must be with us as we go about raising our children. They will rarely learn habits and behaviour which they see us reject, or walk in paths in which we do not walk ourselves. If we do not practice what we preach, then we are simply being ineffective parents. Penelope's web is an old Greek myth that describes a woman who worked at a funeral robe all day long, yet unpicked her work at night so that the work would never be finished. When we as parents try to instruct and raise our children without setting a good example, we are like Penelope: undoing our own hard work. It is as if we build up our children with one hand, yet pull down what we build with the other.

Discussion Questions

1. In what ways do your children already mirror your behaviour and pattern of life (both good and bad)?

2. What aspects of your life have been bad examples to your children that you need to repent of? Do you need to repent of them to your children, as well as to Jesus?

3. What aspects of your life can you build upon and strengthen, to be a better example to your children?

NOTE
1. Sermon 62 'On the Education of Children' from The Works of Dr John Tillotson, Vol. 3 (ed. Thomas Birch, London: Richard Priestley, 1820); modernisation by Ryle, see http://wist.info/tillotson-john/13131/ for details.

CHAPTER 15:
REMEMBER THE POWER OF SIN

Train them, remembering continually the power of sin.

The reason why we should think about this specifically is to guard ourselves against unscriptural expectations. Our children's minds are not a blank sheet of pure white paper, and it is a mistake to think that everything will turn out right if we just follow the right path or use the right means to bring up our children. I warn you plainly that this is not the case.

Of course, it is painful to see how much corruption and evil there is in a young child's heart, and also how soon it begins to bear fruit and show itself. Violent temper tantrums, strong-mindedness, pride, envy, stroppiness, high emotions, laziness, selfishness, deceit, cunning, lying, hypocrisy, a frighteningly good ability to learn what is bad, a painful slowness to learn what is good, a readiness to pretend or do anything in order to get their own way – all these things (or at the very least, some of them) you must be prepared to encounter in children, especially in your own dear flesh and blood. They will creep out in little ways at a very early age. Indeed, it is almost startling to

To be ensnared by sin is the one thing that every person inherits from our first father, Adam.

see just how naturally they seem to spring up. Children require no education or training in how to sin.

But we must not be discouraged and downcast by what we see. We must not think that it is strange and an unusual thing that such little hearts can be so full of sin. To be ensnared by sin is the one thing that every person inherits from our first father, Adam.

When we come into the world, we come with a fallen nature. So instead of being discouraged, it is far better that we become more aware of sin and so more diligent in dealing with it. Let us use every means that, by God's blessing, are most likely to counteract their sinfulness. Let this truth make us more and more careful, inasmuch as we are able, to keep our children out of the way of temptation.

> Let us use every means that, by God's blessing, are most likely to counteract their sinfulness.

Never listen to those who tell you that your children are good, that they are well behaved, and can be trusted. Instead, remind yourself that their hearts are highly flammable with regard to sin. At their very best, they only need a spark to set their sinful desires alight.

Parents are rarely ever too cautious. Remember the natural depravity of your children apart from God's grace, and take care.

Discussion Questions

1. How do you view your children, with regard to sin and temptation?

2. As you read this chapter, how did you feel: defensive, angry, challenged, or comforted, reassured, encouraged?

3. What evidence of sin and sinfulness can you see in your children?

4. What has God given us as parents to counteract sin and sinfulness in our children?

CHAPTER 16:
REMEMBER THE PROMISES OF SCRIPTURE

Train them remembering continually the promises of Scripture.

I mention this simply in order to help you guard against discouragement. As parents, we have a plain promise on our side: 'Train a child in the way he should go, and when he is old he will not turn from it' (Prov. 22:6). Just think what it means to have a promise like this.

The promises of God were the only ray of hope which lifted the hearts of the patriarchs before the Bible was ever written. Enoch, Noah, Abraham, Isaac, Jacob and Joseph all lived with just a few promises, and yet their relationship with God prospered. God's promises are the remedy which in every age has supported and strengthened believers. It is true to say that when we have got a plain bit of Scripture that speaks clearly to us about our situation, we need never be downcast. Parents, when our hearts are aching and we are ready to quit, let's remind ourselves of the truth of Proverbs 22:6, and take great comfort from it.

God's promises are the remedy which in every age has supported and strengthened believers.

Let's start by thinking about who it is that makes this promise. This isn't the promise of a human being, who may lie or change their mind. This is a promise from the King of kings, who is ever faithful and never changes. If God has said He will do something, will He then not do it? If God has spoken something, will He then not keep His word? Of course He will. Nothing is too hard for God to do, and the things that are impossible with humans are possible with God. Put simply, if we never grasp and understand the benefit of this promise, then the fault is in us and not in God.

We must realise that we may not see with our own eyes the result of our careful parenting.

Think carefully about what the promise contains – especially if you are tempted to doubt it. The promise in Proverbs 22:6 speaks of a time when we can be certain that our efforts in bringing up our children shall especially bear fruit in their lives, 'when [they are] old'. There is great comfort in this. But we must realise that we may not see with our own eyes the result of our careful parenting, and that we do not know what blessings and fruitfulness might spring from it, even long after we are gone. It is simply not God's way to give everything at once. 'Later' is the time when He often chooses to work, both in the things of nature and in the things of grace. 'Later' is the season of life when God allows affliction to produce a harvest of righteousness and peace (Heb. 12:11). In the parable of the two sons in Matthew's Gospel, 'later' was the time when the son who refused to work in his father's vineyard repented and went back (Matt. 21:29). And 'later' is the time to which we as parents must look, if we do not see the impact of our parenting straight away; we must sow in hope and plant in hope.

In Ecclesiastes 11:1 we read, 'Cast your bread upon the waters, for after many days you will find it again.' Many children, I do not doubt, will rise up on the last day when Christ returns and bless their parents for bringing them up faithfully, even though they never gave any signs of having benefited from it during their parents' lives. Go forward, then, in faith, and be sure that your efforts are not wasted. In the Old Testament, Elijah was faced with a widow who had lost her son to a tragic illness. Three times he stretched himself out on the boy before God heard his cry and revived the child (1 Kgs. 17:17–23). Take heart from Elijah's example, and persevere.

Discussion Questions

1. Reread Proverbs 22:6. Do you believe the promise of this proverb? Why/why not?

2. What might the fruit of this promise look like in your children? How can you use this to . . .

- motivate you in your parenting?

- fuel your prayers for your children?

CHAPTER 17:
REMEMBER TO PRAY FOR THEM

Lastly, train them with a continual prayer for God's blessing on all you do.

Without the blessing of the Lord, our best endeavours will do no good. God holds the hearts of all people in His hands, and unless He touches the hearts of our children by His Spirit, we will wear ourselves out to no avail. Therefore, we should water the seed that we sow in their hearts and minds with unceasing prayer. We need to remind ourselves that the Lord is far more willing to hear us than we are to pray to Him. He is far more ready to give blessings to us than we are to ask for them – but He loves to be sought and asked for them. So, I set this matter of prayer before you, that it would be the cornerstone and seal of all that you do. I suspect that a child who is the subject of many a prayer is rarely cast away.

We need to remind ourselves that the Lord is far more willing to hear us than we are to pray to Him.

We should regard our children as Jacob did his. In the Old Testament, Jacob and his brother Esau are reunited after a long time apart, so long in fact that Esau asks who all the children are. Jacob explains that they are 'the children God has graciously given your servant' (Gen. 33:5). Likewise, we should have the same attitude that Joseph did about his children. At a similar reunion, Joseph told his father that they were 'the sons God has given me here' (Gen. 48:9).

Count your children, just as the writer of Psalm 127 does, to be 'a heritage from the LORD . . . a reward from him' (Ps. 127:3). With that in mind, humbly yet boldly come to the Lord and ask Him to be gracious and merciful to the children that He Himself has given us. For example, take note of how Abraham intercedes for his son Ishmael, because he loved him: 'If only Ishmael might live under your blessing!' (Gen. 17:18). In another example we can see how Manoah, Samson's father, speaks to the angel of God about how to go about bringing up Samson, when he asks, "what is to be the rule for the boy's life and work?' (Judg. 13:12). Lastly, in Job 1:5 we can see how tenderly Job cared for his children's souls: 'When a period of feasting had run its course, Job would send and have [his children] purified. Early in the morning he would sacrifice a burnt offering for each of them, thinking, "Perhaps my children have sinned and cursed God in their hearts." This was Job's regular custom.'

Parents, if you love your children – bring your children before God regularly in prayer.

Parents, if you love your children, then go and do likewise – bring your children before God regularly in prayer. We cannot name their names before the mercy seat of Jesus too often.

Discussion Questions

1. To what extent is prayer 'the cornerstone and seal of all that you do' as parents?

2. What might Philippians 4:6 look like when applied to your children?

3. What would be the top three things you would want to thank God for, for your children?

4. What would be the top three things you would want to ask God for, for your children?

CONCLUSION: RAISE YOUR CHILDREN FOR GOD

As we conclude, let me once more press upon you the necessity and importance of using every single means in your power, in order to raise your children for heaven.

Now, it is worth acknowledging that God is a sovereign God, and so does all things according to the wisdom of His own will. In Scripture, we do not always see godly parents having godly children, such as harsh Rehoboam, who was the son of the wise king Solomon; or idolatrous Manasseh, who undid the religious reforms of his father, King Hezekiah. But we also know that God is a God who works by means, and we can be certain that if we make light of such means as we have looked at in this book, your children are not likely to turn out well.

If there is no consistent discipleship, education and training at home then, to put it plainly, I fear it will not go well in the end with your children's souls.

Parents, we can bring our children to baptism and welcome them into the family of Christ's church; we can find godly godparents or sponsors to help them as they grow up and help us by their prayers; we might send them to the best of schools, give them the latest youth or children's Bibles, or get them a stack of Christian books, CDs or DVDs; we might fill their heads with all kinds of knowledge. But, even with all of these good things, if there is no consistent discipleship, education and training at home then, to put it plainly, I fear it will not go well in the end with your children's souls. Home is the place where habits are formed. Home is the place where the foundations of our characters are laid. Home is the place where our tastes, likings and opinions are influenced most. Given these truths, I beg of you to see to it that you give careful training to your children in your home. How great would it be if, at the end of our lives, we were able to say to our children something similar to what the seventeenth-century preacher Robert Bolton said to his children on his deathbed that he did not believe one of them would dare to meet him before the tribunal of Christ 'in an unregenerate state.' [1]

I earnestly charge you before God and the Lord Jesus Christ: make every effort to carry out Proverbs 22:6.

Parents, I earnestly charge you before God and the Lord Jesus Christ: make every effort to carry out Proverbs 22:6 and train up your children in the way they should go. I make this charge to you not merely for your children's sakes, but for the sake of your own future comfort and peace. Because, to be honest, it is in our best interests to do this; our own contentment as parents very much depends on it.

It seems that children have forever been the bow from which the sharpest arrows have pierced the human heart. It is as if children have provided the bitterest cups that humanity has ever had to drink, and that children have caused the saddest tears that humankind has ever had to shed. Plenty of people from the Bible would testify to this, such as Adam, Jacob, and King David. There are no sorrows on earth like those which children have brought on their parents. So, we must take heed of what the Bible urges us or else our own neglect of Scripture will store up sorrow for us in our old age. Take heed, or else we will be brought to tears from the trouble caused by a thankless child, especially when we are weak and tired in our old age.

Who doesn't long for our children to be a fulfilment to us, and be a source of vitality to us in our later years? Which would we rather: our children become a blessing or a curse; bring joy or sorrow? Would we rather our children were like Jacob's repentant son Judah, or his incestuous son Reuben? Would we hope for them to be like Ruth, who stuck with her mother-in-Law Naomi, or like Orpah who abandoned her and returned home? I'm sure that none of us would want our children to be like Noah's sons, who did some shameful things, or like Rebekah's children, who did things that even made her weary of life. If we want the best and not the worst from our children, then train them while they are young in the right way God has given us.

> Who doesn't long for our children to be a fulfilment to us, and be a source of vitality to us in our later years?

And as for me, I will close with my own prayer to God for all who read this: that He might show us all the value of our own souls. Failure to grasp the importance of nurturing a healthy relationship with God is one of the main reasons why baptism has become a mere ritual, and why Christian parenting in biblical values has become despised and disregarded. Too often parents neglect their own relationship with Jesus, and so they neglect their children's walk with Him, too. They do not realise the tremendous difference between their children's natural standing before God and the standing that only comes by the grace of Jesus, and therefore they are content to leave them alone.

I long for parents to raise their children for God, for Christ, and for eternity.

I pray that the Lord would show us all just how much sin is something that God hates and cannot stand. I pray this so that we will grieve the sins of our children and, as if they were brands in a fire, strive to grab hold of them and pull them out of the flames of their own sinfulness and folly.

I also pray that God will show us all how precious Christ is, and what a mighty and complete work He has done for us to give us our salvation. When we grasp this, we will surely use every means to bring our children to Jesus, that they may have eternal life through Him.

And I pray that God would show us all our need of the Holy Spirit to renew, sanctify, and bring life to our souls. Then I am certain we will urge our children to always pray for the Holy Spirit to be in them and with them, and to never rest until He has come down into their hearts with power, and made them a new creation in Christ.

Lastly, I pray that the Lord would grant all of this so that we might have a good hope that we will indeed train up our children well: train them well for this life, and train them well for the life to come; train them well for earth, and train them well for heaven.

I long for parents to raise their children for God, for Christ, and for eternity.

Discussion Questions

1. What is your number one goal, aim or desire for your children? Has it changed while reading this book?

2. What legacy do you long to leave for your children and your children's children?

3. At the end of your children's lives, what do you hope for?

NOTE

1. See http://wesley.nnu.edu/index.php?id=490

a division of 10 of those.com

10Publishing is the publishing house of **10ofThose**.
It is committed to producing quality Christian
resources that are biblical and accessible.

www.10ofthose.com is our online retail arm selling
thousands of quality books at discounted prices.
We also service many church bookstalls
and can help your church to set up a bookstall.
Single and bulk purchases welcome.

For information contact: **sales@10ofthose.com**
or check out our website: **www.10ofthose.com**